Love and Logicisms

Love and Logicisms

by Jim Fay and Charles Fay, Ph.D.

Love and Logic® INSTITUTE, Inc.
800-338-4065 · www.loveandlogic.com

America's Parenting Experts®

The Love and Logic Institute, Inc.
2207 Jackson Street, Golden, CO 80401-2300
www.loveandlogic.com

First edition
First printing, 2001
Printed in the United States of America

ISBN 1-930429-14-2

Library of Congress Number: 2001086944

BOOK PRODUCTION AND DESIGN:

Carol Thomas, project coordinator

Michael Snell, Shade of the Cottonwood, Topeka, KS
cover design and interior design

Paula Niedrach Botkin, illustrations

Wise Words adapted from

Love and Logic Magic:
When Kids Leave You Speechless

LOVE AND LOGIC®

Easy to Learn

Life Changing

Raises Responsible Kids

INTRODUCTION

IF YOU'VE EVER EXPERIENCED THE THRILL OF ATTENDING a Love and Logic seminar with Jim Fay, Foster W. Cline, M.D., or Charles Fay, Ph.D. you know that their speeches are riddled with thought capturing insights about kids. These spontaneous truths about kids flow so fast that it's difficult to take notes fast enough to capture them all.

Each of these "Wise Words" not only tugs at both heart and mind, but also has the power to change lives for the better.

It is with pride that we have selected 100 of these mind-bending truths to enhance your understanding of those wonderful creatures who inhabit our homes and serve to enrich our lives by being part of our families. Please accept each of the "Wise Words" offered in this powerful little book as our gift to you and as our contribution to a richer life with your children.

— THE EDITORS OF LOVE AND LOGIC

Jim Fay is one of America's most sought-after presenters in the area of parenting and school discipline. His background includes 31 years as a teacher and administrator, 20 as a professional consultant and public speaker, and many years as the parent of three children.

Jim is internationally recognized as a speaker and consultant to schools, parent organizations, counselors, mental health organizations, and the U.S. Military. He is the author of more than 100 articles, books, audios, CD's, and videotapes on parenting and discipline. His infectious spirit and sense of humor has made him a popular personality on radio and television talk shows.

Dr. Charles Fay is a parent,

School Psychologist, and consultant to schools, parent groups, and mental health professionals across the United States. His expertise in developing and teaching practical discipline and behavior management strategies has been refined through work with severely disturbed children and adolescents in school, hospital, and community settings.

WHAT IS LOVE AND LOGIC®

Love allows children to grow through their mistakes.

Logic allows children to live with the consequences of their choices.

THE LOVE AND LOGIC PROCESS

1. *Shared control: Gain control by giving away the control you don't need.*

2. *Shared thinking and decision-making: Provide opportunities for the child to do the greatest amount of thinking and decision-making.*

3. *Equal shares of consequences with empathy: An absence of anger causes a child to think and learn from his/her mistakes.*

4. *Maintain the child's self concept: Increased self-concept leads to improved behavior and improved achievement.*

*Wise parents are consistently available
to listen to their children when
they hurt, are disappointed, or need advice.
They teach their children how to approach
them with sincere concerns, and they
are always willing to discuss problems in
a calm, loving manner.*

Love and Logic Institute, Inc. • www.lovoondluyic.com

*Wise parents never try
to convince kids that their
decisions are fair.*

Love and Logic Institute, Inc. • www.loveandlogic.com

Chores are the basic building blocks of pride and feelings of being loved and needed by one's family. Kids who have this at home don't need to find it in a cult or street gang.

Love and Logic Institute, Inc. • www.loveandlogic.com

Do not pay your kids for completing their chores.

Love and Logic Institute, Inc. • www.loveandlogic.com

When kids say, "Mary's mom doesn't make her do chores," wise parents smile and say, "Well that's really sad for Mary. Aren't you glad I love you enough to expect more of you?"

Chores represent the basic
foundation for cooperation
with parents and other
authority figures.

Chores are so important to lifelong success that wise parents win the battle over them at all costs—for both themselves and their children.

Wise parents delay consequences until they have time to talk to others and put together a "watertight" plan. These plans teach resistant kids that their parents are so powerful that they can handle them without breaking a sweat—and so loving that they can discipline with sadness instead of anger.

Love and Logic Institute, Inc. • www.loveandlogic.com

*Every time we lecture a child about what
he or she has learned, or say something like,
"Now, have you learned your lesson?"
we rub salt into the wounds and damage the
parent-child relationship. Kids learn most from
consequences when we keep our mouths shut
and let the consequence be the "bad guy."*

*Wise parents don't dignify the ridiculous
by offering factual information.
There's nothing wrong with a child that
an arguing parent can't make worse.*

Love and Logic Institute, Inc. • www.loveandlogic.com

Wise parents know that their kids may someday choose their nursing home.

*Wise parents know the difference
between a manipulating child and one
who is hurting and desperately needs
them to listen and understand.*

*Kids who don't feel listened-to and
understood by their parents tend
to search for these feelings in
other places—in gangs—in cults—in
drugs—in sex—etc.*

Love and Logic Institute, Inc. • www.loveandlogic.com

*Listening and using empathy
is more important
than "fixing" the problem.*

Kids are usually more likely to talk about difficult issues if they are interacting with us over some other fun activity. Next time your child seems upset, play a game with him, start a woodworking project, or bake some cookies together. You might be surprised what comes out!

Love and Logic Institute, Inc. • www.loveandlogic.com

Wise parents know how to give guidance while keeping responsibility for the problem squarely on their children's shoulders.

Love and Logic Institute, Inc. • www.loveandlogic.com

Wise parents know that kids only threaten to starve themselves. If this were anything but a hollow threat, there would be no adults alive today to be tricked by these hollow threats.

Wise parents know that the battles fought with children about eating eventually become eating disorders after kids leave the family.
(The battles never end. They start out at the conscious level and later move to the subconscious level.)

Wise parents don't allow words to gain shock value.

Love and Logic Institute, Inc. • www.loveandlogic.com

*Lectures and threats make
the problem worse. Wise parents take
the fun out of swearing by
encouraging the use of the "dirty" word
in some other place.*

When kids insist on swearing around their parents, their parents fall back on the "energy drain" principle: Swearing drains energy from the family, but there's nothing like your kids cleaning the toilets or staying home from the amusement park to charge it up!

Saying "No" to a $200 pair
of sneakers does not constitute
child abuse.

Never expect that giving concessions will bring gratitude. Concessions made to demanding kids rob them of the opportunity to learn respectfulness, responsibility, and how to earn what they want.

To avoid a fight with your kids,
tell them what you will provide, not
what they have to do.

Love and Logic Institute, Inc. • www.loveandlogic.com

*The best person to answer the
question "but why?" is the
person asking it. Wise parents
respond to "But why?" with
"And why do you think?"*

*Wise parents recognize
the difference between genuine
curiosity and manipulation.*

Wise parents know an angry,
"'Cause I said so!" makes life for them
and their children a whole lot worse.

Love and Logic Institute, Inc. • www.loveandlogic.com

*Love and Logic parents become
more like a cloud
than a brick wall in the face of
attacks or arguments.*

Love and Logic Institute, Inc. • www.loveandlogic.com

Parents who try to be
the "brick wall" soon have and
feel many battle scars.

Wise parents don't allow
themselves to be drawn into arguments
over their kids' body language.

*The more we lecture, threaten,
and yell about nasty looks, the more
our children learn that
nonverbal barbs are an effective way
of controlling others and
getting an entertaining show of
frustration and anger.*

Love and Logic Institute, Inc. • www.loveandlogic.com

Never let a manipulating child
see you sweat.

*It's simple. Don't fight
with your kids over nasty looks
if they are actually doing
what you want! Just say,
"I know you don't like this,
but thanks for doing it for me
anyway. I love you."*

*Wise parents don't do
special things for kids who treat
them like barnyard waste.*

*When you use an effective technique,
be thankful when your kids get mad and
throw fits. This is how you will know
your approach is working. Stick with it!
In the long run, you'll be glad you did!*

Love and Logic Institute, Inc. • www.loveandlogic.com

Wise parents encourage
their kids to go first class
on their own money.

Never give a kid the bad news about the cost of something, if someone else will do it for you. Why? Children, like adults, are always angriest with the messenger.

*Wise parents know that strong
family relationships and good parenting
are far more powerful and longer
lasting influences than peer pressure.*

Love and Logic Institute, Inc. • www.loveandlogic.com

Doing the right thing for your kids
often feels terrible at the time.
The results and good feelings come
much later.

Parents who battle with their kids
over friendship choices create
teenagers who sneak around
behind their backs.

Love and Logic Institute, Inc. • www.loveandlogic.com

*One of the most powerful things
you can do is to get your kids' friends
to fall in love with you.*

*Parents are wise to worry
about the type of "education" their kids
are getting on the Internet.*

There are no things more powerful than quiet, loving, or silly moments between us and our kids. These moments can only flower when the distractions and temptations of our TVs and computer screens are switched off. Try experimenting with a TV-free and computer-free weekend. You may be pleasantly surprised!

Love and Logic Institute, Inc. • www.loveandlogic.com

Without saying a word, we constantly show our kids what we believe they can be. They will either live up to our highest expectations—or down to our greatest fears.

Love and Logic Institute, Inc. • www.loveandlogic.com

*It's really hard to surf the Net
without a surfboard. Wise parents remove the
computer as soon as it becomes
an object of constant hassles or conflict.*

When a child says, "I hate you," they are really saying, "I'm doing everything I can to manipulate you and it isn't working! I want my way!"

The only throne a child should sit on
is in the bathroom. Kids always feel safer
and more loved when Mom and Dad
are queen and king in a loving, gentle way.

*Wise parents aren't afraid of their
kids getting mad at them. They understand
that children can hate what their parents do—
while still loving their parents very much.
Wise parents also teach their kids
that it is OK to be mad but not OK to
hurt others with words or actions.*

Love and Logic Institute, Inc. • www.loveandlogic.com

Anger and frustration feed misbehavior. Wise parents understand that sadness is a much better teacher than anger.

Wise parents wait until they are
calm and have a solid plan
before delivering consequences.

Wise parents realize that it is more difficult to make good decisions when issues center around their own childhood fears or pains. Wise parents don't allow OTHER parents' rules to dictate how they run their own homes.

Wise parents know that kids will
use guilt only if it works on their parents.
And, wise parents never allow guilt to
guide their parenting.

Wise parents remember:
"Never let your kids see you sweat!"

Love and Logic Institute, Inc. • www.loveandlogic.com

*Wise parents know that good discipline
and logical consequences still work,
even when their kids roll their eyes and say,
"I don't care if you do that."*

Love and Logic Institute, Inc. • www.loveandlogic.com

*Wise parents never waste words trying
to talk their kids into caring.*

Love and Logic Institute, Inc. • www.loveandlogic.com

When a child says, "I don't care if you do that," the wise parent enthusiastically responds, "Oh thank goodness! That makes it a lot easier for both of us."

Love and Logic Institute, Inc. • www.loveandlogic.com

Parents who use larger and more meaningful consequences when misbehaviors just begin, find that they have to use fewer consequences in the long run. They also notice that their kids are happier and better behaved.

Parents who use smaller and less meaningful
consequences when misbehaviors begin,
find that they have to use many
more consequences—and larger ones
in the long run.
They also notice that their kids are resentful
and poorly behaved.

Wise parents know that most real world consequences come without warnings. They parent in a way that creates a voice inside of their children's heads. This voice says, "If I make a bad choice, something bad or even dangerous could happen—without any warnings."

Wise parents don't hesitate to get professional help when their kids show signs of depression.

*Therapists who only work
with the child—without working
with the parents as well—usually
have poorer results.*

Children who learn that temper tantrums
work become adults who use
them often. Wise parents take control
of this problem when the child is
still small enough to carry.

Love and Logic Institute, Inc. • www.loveandlogic.com

How parents handle toddler temper tantrums determines how their children will deal with authority figures, disappointments, and anger for the rest of their lives.

*All kids experiment with both nice
and nasty behavior. Wise parents
show their kids that sweetness gets you
a lot—nastiness gets you nothing.*

Wise parents know that anger and
frustration feed misbehavior.

Wise parents show their kids
that nowhere is safe
from the "Uh Oh Song."

Love and Logic Institute, Inc. • www.loveandlogic.com

When drugs and alcohol are concerned, what a parent doesn't know CAN kill their kids.

A Common Parenting Myth:
Parents should never search their
children's rooms.

Love and Logic Institute, Inc. • www.loveandlogic.com

*Denial is more lethal
than a gunshot wound
to the head!*

Drug use is a symptom of deeper problems that must be addressed with the help of a qualified professional.

Wise parents know that it is good
for kids to go "first class" as a result of
their OWN efforts.

Love and Logic Institute, Inc. • www.loveandlogic.com

*While in the heat of emotion,
it's a very poor time to make any kind
of decision.*

Love and Logic Institute, Inc. • www.loveandlogic.com

Smart parents know how to set limits by agreeing with their kids: "I agree! Those sneakers are great. I'll pay $29.95 toward them. Won't it be great when you've earned enough money to cover the rest?"

Wise parents know that the best way to get their kids to hate each other is to make them shake hands and say, "I'm sorry."

Love and Logic Institute, Inc. • www.loveandlogic.com

*Sibling spats are excellent learning opportunities for children.
How better to practice the skills necessary for getting along with a tough teacher, a demanding boss, or your future spouse?*

Wise parents realize that yelling,
"Stop fighting!" is about as effective as
fighting fires with a squirt gun.

Love and Logic Institute, Inc. • www.loveandlogic.com

There is no case of sibling rivalry that can't be made worse by a strong dose of parental frustration, anger, or worry.

*Wise stepparents occasionally need to say
"You're right! I'm not your real mom.
But I do respect you too much to argue.
I'll do something about this after
I've talked with your dad (or mom)."*

*The world's most powerful people
focus the vast majority of their energy on
what they can control beyond a shadow
of a doubt—their own thoughts,
feelings, and actions.*

*Control is a lot like love and respect.
The more we give, the more we receive.*

*The more kids are able to
control adults through manipulation,
the more out of control
they feel—and are!*

Love and Logic Institute, Inc. • www.loveandlogic.com

*Wise parents empathize with feelings
but don't excuse misbehavior.*

Unless your spouse has done
something downright abusive
or neglectful, it is always best
to support them in the eyes
of the child.

Wise parents recognize
"guilt trips" from their kids,
and they never give in to this type
of manipulation.

*Wise parents know that
the better they take care of themselves,
the more love they will have
for their children.*

Love and Logic Institute, Inc. • www.loveandlogic.com

Wise parents know
that NOT getting one's way
from time to time is actually
good practice for life!
Children who are always
protected from being upset become
always upset adults.

Never reason with a drunk.

Love and Logic Institute, Inc. • www.loveandlogic.com

Angry people need three things:
Empathy, space, and time to cool down.
The only person who can really
calm an angry person is that person.

Love and Logic Institute, Inc. • www.loveandlogic.com

*In boredom are the seeds of creativity.
Wise parents allow their kids to get
bored, and they help them channel this
feeling into creative discoveries.*

*The more we entertain kids, the more
they will start to believe they
need to be entertained.*

More is not always better.
Exciting, entertaining activities
are great fun, but wise parents
also know that quiet times
are just as important!

Love and Logic Institute, Inc. • www.loveandlogic.com

*The ability to tolerate boredom
and to entertain oneself are essential
life skills. Like any other abilities,
practice makes perfect.*

*Wise parents never try something new
with their kids before they've asked
themselves, "How might my child react?"
and "What might go wrong with my plan?"
Successful parents find the holes and
plug them—before they launch the boat!*

Wise parents hand the
"boredom problem" right back to their
kids in a loving way.
In response to, "This is boooring!"
smart parents ask with empathy,
"What are you going to do?"

Wise parents know that arguments
are not requests to hear parental wisdom.
Instead, they are designed to weaken
parent's resolve and get one's way.

It is easier and more effective to tell kids WHEN they CAN do something—instead of telling them "No" or lecturing.

Love and Logic Institute, Inc. • www.loveandlogic.com

The best technique in the world won't work if your kids believe that you won't back your words with actions.

Wise parents know that
doing the right thing won't guarantee
a happy kid.

*Wise parents remember
their civic responsibility to report
unlawful activities.*

Additional copies of this book are available through

Love and Logic Institute, Inc.
2207 Jackson Street
Golden, Colorado 80401-2300

Call or visit our Website to order our complete catalog
of stress-free parenting and teaching titles.

1-800-338-4065

www.loveandlogic.com

With Charles Fay, Ph.D.

Love and Logic Magic for Early Childhood
Love and Logic Magic: When Kids Leave You Speechless
Calming the Chaos
Hope for Underachieving Kids

By Charles Fay, Ph.D.

Oh Great! What Do I Do Now?
Angry & Oppositional Students: Calming Classrooms with Love and Logic

Love and Logic Seminars

Jim and Charles Fay, Ph.D. present
Love and Logic seminars and personal appearances
for both parents and educators in
many cities each year.

For more information,
contact Love and Logic Institute, Inc. at:

1-800-338-4065

or visit our Website:

www.loveandlogic.com